RESTORED
LEADER GUIDE

RESTORED
FINDING REDEMPTION IN OUR MESS

Restored: Finding Redemption in Our Mess
978-1-5018-2292-6
978-1-5018-2293-3 *eBook*

Restored: Leader Guide
978-1-5018-2294-0
978-1-5018-2295-7 *eBook*

Restored: DVD
978-1-5018-2296-4

Restored: Youth Study Book
978-1-5018-2303-9
978-1-5018-2304-6 *eBook*

For more information, visit www.AbingdonPress.com.

From Tom Berlin

Defying Gravity: Break Free from the Culture of More
6 Decisions That Will Change Your Life
6 Ways We Encounter God
6 Things We Should Know About God

From Tom Berlin and Lovett H. Weems Jr.

Bearing Fruit: Ministry with Real Results
High Yield: Seven Disciplines of the Fruitful Leader
Overflow: Increase Worship Attendance & Bear More Fruit

TOM BERLIN

RESTORED

FINDING REDEMPTION IN OUR MESS

Leader Guide
by Clara Welch

Abingdon Press / Nashville

RESTORED
FINDING REDEMPTION IN OUR MESS
LEADER GUIDE

Copyright © 2016 Abingdon Press
All rights reserved.

This book is printed on elemental chlorine-free paper.

978-1-5018-2294-0

16 17 18 19 20 21 22 23 24 25 — 10 9 8 7 6 5 4 3 2 1
MANUFACTURED IN THE UNITED STATES OF AMERICA

CONTENTS

To the Leader 7

1. This Is a Real Mess. 13

2. Who Left This Mess?. 23

3. Bless This Mess 33

4. No Messing Around 41

5. Address This Mess. 49

6. The Message in the Mess 57

Notes 64

TO THE LEADER

Welcome! Thank you for accepting the invitation to serve as a facilitator for this 6-session study. You and your group of learners will journey together toward a restored relationship with God and with other people.

In his book *Restored*, Tom Berlin writes in depth about the "mess" in our lives that covers and hides the image of God within us. He guides readers through the process of identifying and accepting responsibility for the mess, and then offers guidance on ways to address the mess and experience transformation and new life in Christ.

This six-session study for adults makes use of the following components:

- Tom Berlin's book *Restored*
- this Leader Guide
- a DVD

Participants in the study will need a copy of *Restored* and a Bible. It will be helpful if participants also have notebooks, paper, or an electronic equivalent. If possible, make arrangements for participants

7

to get copies of the book ahead of time so they may read Chapter 1 before the first session.

Using This Guide with Your Group

Scripture tells us that where two or three are gathered together, we can be assured of the presence of the Holy Spirit working in and through all those gathered. As you prepare to lead, pray for that presence and expect that you will experience it.

Because no two groups are alike, this guide has been designed to give you as study leader some flexibility and choice in tailoring the sessions for your group. The session format is listed below.

In the book and videos, participants will discover a rich offering of information presented in an accessible way. As study leader, you will want to tailor your session activities to the needs and interests of your particular group, as well as to the timeframe you have available.

Session Format

Planning the Session
    Session Goals
    Biblical Foundation
    Before the Session

Getting Started
    Opening Activities
    Opening Prayer

Learning Together
    Video Study and Discussion
    Bible Study and Discussion
    Book Study and Discussion

Wrapping Up
    Closing Activity
    Closing Prayer

Helpful Hints

Preparing for the Session

- Pray for the leading of the Holy Spirit as you prepare for the study. Pray for discernment for yourself and for each member of the study group.
- Before each session, familiarize yourself with the content. Read the session chapter again and watch the video segment.
- Read "Before the Session" several days in advance of the session. Some ideas will need advance preparation.
- Choose the session elements you will use during the group session, including the specific discussion questions you plan to cover. Be prepared, however, to adjust the session as group members interact and as questions arise. Prepare carefully, but allow space for the Holy Spirit to move through the group members and through you as facilitator.
- Secure a TV and DVD player in advance.
- Prepare the space where the session will be held so that it will enhance the learning process. Ideally, group members should be seated around a table or in a circle so that all can see one another. Moveable chairs are best, because the group may form pairs or smaller groups for discussion.
- Bring a supply of Bibles for those who forget to bring their own. Having a variety of translations is helpful.
- For each session you will also need a chalkboard and chalk, a dry-erase board and markers, or an easel with paper and markers.

Shaping the Learning Environment

- Create a climate of openness, encouraging group members to participate as they feel comfortable. Remember that some people will jump right in with answers and comments, while others need time to process what is being discussed.

- If you notice that some group members never seem to enter the conversation, ask them if they have thoughts to share. Give everyone a chance to talk, but keep the conversation moving. Moderate to prevent a few individuals from doing all the talking.
- Communicate the importance of group discussions and group exercises.
- If no one answers at first during discussions, do not be afraid of a silence. Count silently to ten; then say something such as, "Would anyone like to go first?" If no one responds, venture an answer yourself and ask for comments.
- Model openness as you share with the group. Group members will follow your example. If you limit your sharing to a surface level, others will do the same.
- Encourage multiple answers or responses before moving on.
- To help continue a discussion and give it greater depth, ask, "Why?" or "Why do you believe that?" or "Can you say more about that?"
- Affirm others' responses with comments such as "Great" or "Thanks" or "Good insight"—especially if this is the first time someone has spoken during the group session.
- Monitor your own contributions. If you are doing most of the talking, back off so that you do not train the group to listen rather than speak up.
- Remember that you do not have all the answers. Your job is to keep the discussion going and encourage participation.

Managing the Session

- Begin and end on time. If a session is running longer than expected, get consensus from the group before continuing beyond the agreed-upon ending time.

- Involve group members in various aspects of the group session, such as playing the DVD, saying prayers, or reading the Scripture.
- Note that some sessions may call for breaking into smaller groups or pairs. This gives everyone a chance to speak and participate fully. Mix up the groups; don't let the same people pair up for every activity.
- The study will be most successful if group members treat one another with respect and are willing to listen to opinions that differ from their own. Work to ensure that the study offers a safe space for exploring the topic of restoration and reconciliation with God.
- Ask the group to covenant together to observe a policy of confidentiality.

1

THIS IS A REAL MESS

Planning the Session

Session Goals

Through conversation, activities, and reflection, participants will:

- Explore what it means to be made in the image of God;
- Consider the damaging consequences of sin;
- Examine our reluctance to face our sin;
- Discover ways to begin the process of restoring the beauty of God's image in our lives.

Biblical Foundation

- Luke 18:9-14
- Genesis 1:27

Before the Session

- Set up a table in the room with nametags, markers, Bibles, extra copies of *Restored*, a small stack of printer or notebook paper, and pencils.
- Have available a chalkboard and chalk, a dry-erase board and markers, or large sheets of paper and markers to record participants' responses during the session.
- In preparation for the "Leading into the Study" activity, write this quotation from Luke 18:11 on the board or a large sheet of paper: "God, I thank you that I'm not like everyone else." Leave space below for writing group responses.

Getting Started

Opening Activities

Greet participants as they arrive and invite them to make a nametag. Have a supply of Bibles and extra copies of *Restored* on hand for those who may have forgotten to bring one. Also be sure that each participant has paper and pen or pencil, or the electronic equivalent, as these will be used throughout the session.

Introductions

Introduce yourself and share why you are excited about facilitating this study of *Restored*.

If you sense that the participants in your group do not know each other well, allow time for them to introduce themselves and share something about their relationship with the church—for example, the name of a church group to which they belong, a mission project they support, or a particular worship service they attend. Extend a special welcome to those people who does not regularly attend your church and invite them to worship at your church if they do not have a church home.

14

Leading into the Study

Read or ask someone to read Luke 18:11-12. Write responses to the following questions on the sheet you prepared before class.

- Note the general categories: "crooks, evildoers, adulterers… tax collector." What modern-day examples might we include to prove our point to God that we are not like everyone else? *(Some examples are bank robbers, hijackers, kidnappers. Record the first four or five responses from the group.)*
- Note the Pharisee's examples of fasting and tithing to prove his righteousness before God. What modern-day examples of our own righteousness might we point out to God? *(Some examples are attending worship, teaching Sunday school, singing in the choir.)*

Housekeeping

- Share any necessary information about your meeting space and parking.
- Let participants know you will be faithful to the time and encourage everyone to arrive on time.
- Encourage participants to read the upcoming chapter each week and do any "homework" that may be suggested.
- Suggest that participants may want to have a notebook or an electronic equivalent for use during the study. Explain that it may be used for recording questions and insights as they read the book and attend the sessions. It may also be used for writing reflections as they consider the topic of restoration.
- Stress the importance of confidentiality within the group. Ask participants to covenant together that they will respect a policy of confidentiality.

Opening Prayer

Holy God, it amazes us that you love us enough to have created us in your image. We are sorry that we allow sin to damage the beauty of your image within us. Guide us along this journey. Help us to clearly see the sin in our own lives. Grant us courage and wisdom as we accept the mess we have made. Show us how to take steps to clean up the mess. Thank you for the opportunity to be restored into a right relationship with you. Amen.

Learning Together

Video Study and Discussion

Introduce the video by inviting participants to first imagine a showroom of new cars, then to imagine a junkyard filled with cars that have been in accidents. Note that the setting for this video is a junkyard, and Tom Berlin compares a car that has been messed up in a wreck to our lives that are messed up by sin.

Ask participants to make note of any of Tom's comments that describe their own lives or situations as they watch the video. (This video is a bit shorter than the others—about five minutes rather than seven to ten minutes—to allow more time for first-session introductions and housekeeping.)

After viewing the video, ask:

- How does Tom Berlin define *sin* in the video?

These next two questions are very personal. Remind participants that sharing is completely voluntary. You may want to share a response to one or both questions to help start the conversation. If no one wants to share, then allow a few minutes for participants to write down responses for further reflection. Ask:

- Which of Tom Berlin's comments about the life of an automobile also describe your life?
- Can you think of some part of your life or some relationship you have that really is in need of attention and repair?

Bible Study and Discussion

Read, or invite someone to read, Luke 18:9-14. Ask:

- What was the attitude of the Pharisee when he prayed?
- What was the attitude of the tax collector when he prayed?
- Which one was "justified" or granted a right relationship with God after his prayer? Why? *(*You may want to invite participants to refer to the section in *Restored* titled "The Pharisee and the Tax Collector" for more information about what it means to be justified before God.*)*

Close this discussion by calling attention to Tom Berlin's point that our encounters with God should leave us "with a sense of humility or gratitude for God's grace." God's work of restoration in our lives is hindered by our pride and self-righteousness.

Book Study and Discussion

Review Tom Berlin's opening remarks about the painting in the Sistine Chapel. Invite participants to respond to these two observations about the painting:

- "The image consists of two hands. The one on the right is the hand of God, reaching toward Adam, trying to make contact and infuse him with life. The hand on the left belongs to Adam, who reaches feebly back, fingers slack, as if thinking: *I don't know. I kind of maybe want what God is offering. Sort of. Not sure. I hope to get around to it. I need to think about it awhile.*"
- "When you stand in the Sistine Chapel and look at the piece, your eye will inevitably compare the figure of God in active pursuit to the figure of Adam in passive repose."

Created in the Image of God

Read Genesis 1:27—"God created humanity in God's own image, in the divine image God created them, male and female God created them." Ask:

- What does it mean to be created in God's image?

Share these observations:

The face of a newborn child is full of hope. It is a mixture of innocence and potential.

You look at his eyes, let his fingers curl around your own and feel his warmth. This child is, in the words of the Bible, *very good*, and it feels like anything is possible for him. The miracle of the child that you hold makes it easier to believe that God exists. Genesis tells us that we are *made in God's image*. The goodness of God is impressed on our souls.

Every parent knows the rapid changes that children exhibit as they grow up. That innocent baby soon becomes a child standing next to a broken cookie jar, sheepishly making excuses. As children grow older, the issues become more complex. Their goodness is very good, a source of great pride and appreciation. However, their capacity for bad can be disappointing. This is the human condition. It is easy to become so fixated on the bad that we forget what is intrinsic to the human soul. That is not our opinion, but the observation of God at creation. You and the people around you are created in God's image, and that is *very good*.

Offer this instruction to the group: List three to five ways that you see the goodness of God reflected in your life. Allow a few minutes for participants to do this individually, then invite volunteers to share from their lists and record responses on the board or a large sheet of paper.

Looking at Sin

Note Tom Berlin's comment: "The grime of sin covers us and hides the great beauty God intended for us and the world to enjoy."

Invite a volunteer to share actor Bill Murray's comments about the human condition.

Invite someone to read Luke 6:42.

Invite someone else to read John 8:7.

Note that in these Scriptures, Jesus is warning us against self-righteousness. Paul echoed Jesus by writing, "All have sinned and fall short of God's glory" (Romans 3:23).

Share this description of sin: "A sin is an action or attitude that is in conflict with God's desire for our lives. Humans commit sins so frequently that we come to realize that our problem is not one specific sin we regret, but that our lives are in a state of sin. This is the conflict found in the human story. We want to know God's presence, but we also want to do whatever we desire. The result is alienation from the One who created us."

Note Tom Berlin's point in his discussion of "The Pharisee and the Tax Collector" that "admission of a bad life is the first step in finding a new life." Invite participants to share responses to the following questions in groups of two to four people. Remind participants that sharing is voluntary and all responses will be kept in confidence. Ask:

- What actions and attitudes in your life are in conflict with God's desire for you?
- What situations make you most mindful of this tension between following your own desires and following God's will for your life?
- What parts of God's beautiful and loving image within you are hidden by sin?

Call the group back together. Invite participants to turn to the section of the chapter titled "Stop Trying to Manage Your Sin." Ask:

19

- What are some of the strategies people use to manage their sin? *(denial and admiring the problem)*
- What feelings motivate these strategies? Why do you think we experience these feelings? How should we handle them?
- How do you feel about sharing your struggles with people you trust?
- How do you feel when others share their struggles with you?

Restoring God's Image within You

Say: The good news of Jesus Christ is the fact that our sinfulness is not the end of the story. Paul goes on to say, "but all are treated as righteous freely by his grace because of a ransom that was paid by Christ Jesus" (Romans 3:24). In his story of the Pharisee and the tax collector, Jesus invites each of us to cry out as the tax collector did, "God, show mercy to me, a sinner" (Luke 18:13).

Share this quotation from *Restored*: "If we can own our sin, we can get rid of our old strategies for sin management." Ask:

- What does it mean to "own our sin"?
- How do ownership of and honesty about our sin and our need for God's mercy open the door to restoration and healing with God?
- What are helpful strategies for dealing with our sin?

Wrapping Up

Closing Activity

In the chapter, Tom Berlin notes the restoration process that took place to restore the Sistine Chapel painting to its original beauty. An art restorer may consider these three questions when restoring a work of art:

- What is covering the original work?
- How severe is the problem?

- What must I do to restore the beauty of the masterpiece?

Invite participants to set aside time for personal reflection during the week and to consider these questions as they relate to the image of God within themselves.

Closing Prayer

Merciful God, we thank you for your gift of forgiveness that invites and leads us into a restored relationship with you. Grant us the courage to look honestly at our lives and the wisdom to recognize the sin that keeps us from being the people you have created us to be. Guide us as we journey together and share together. Thank you for the promise of a restored relationship with you. Amen.

2

WHO LEFT THIS MESS?

Planning the Session

Session Goals

Through conversation, activities, and reflection, participants will begin to:

- Discover the meaning of prevenient grace;
- Consider why our lives sometimes end up in a mess;
- Accept the invitation to a restored relationship with God;
- Imagine how our changed lives also bring about change in our families and communities.

Biblical Foundation

- Luke 19:1-10

Before the Session

- Set up a table in the room with nametags, markers, Bibles, extra copies of *Restored*, a small stack of printer or notebook paper, and pencils.
- Have available a chalkboard and chalk, a dry-erase board and markers, or large sheets of paper and markers to record participants' responses during the session.
- Write the heading "Turning Points" on the board or a large sheet of paper and display it in the room. This will be used during the discussion of both the video and the book.
- Make multiple copies of the following questions to distribute when you break the group into smaller groups.
  - o How did the person asking for healing approach Jesus?
  - o How do you think the person felt about approaching Jesus?
  - o How did Jesus respond?

Getting Started

Opening Activities

Greet participants as they arrive and invite them to make a nametag. Have a supply of Bibles and extra copies of *Restored* on hand for those who may have forgotten to bring one. Also be sure that each participant has paper and pen or pencil.

If there are newcomers to the group, introduce yourself and allow a brief time for participants to introduce themselves. Remind participants to covenant together that they will respect a policy of confidentiality.

Leading into the Study

Remind participants of the story in *Restored* about the man who was locked out of his home on a cold morning when he went outside to get the newspaper.

Invite participants to share quick examples of experiences that left them asking, "How did I get here?" or "How did this happen?" The examples may be serious or humorous. If your group is large, invite participants to share in pairs or small groups, or limit the number of participants who share to four or five. Close this activity by noting:

- Sometimes we are responsible for the mess in which we find ourselves.
- Sometimes we are victims of circumstances.
- Always God is ready to help us and offer us a new and transformed life.

Opening Prayer

Loving God, we confess that we do not always follow your will for our lives. When we stray from the life you call us to live, we allow your divine image within us to get lost. Because of our sin and our wrongdoing, our lives sometimes end up in a mess. We thank you, merciful God, that you come to us in the mess. We thank you for your forgiveness that offers us a way out of the mess and offers us a new opportunity to follow your will. Grant us the courage of Zacchaeus, who climbed a tree to see you more clearly. Let us be like Zacchaeus and accept the new life you offer us. Amen.

Learning Together

Video Study and Discussion

Introduce the video by saying: In this video Tom Berlin explains the meaning of prevenient grace. Four individuals who have participated in the program Celebrate Recovery share how their lives were once a mess, and how, through God's grace, they have experienced healing and are now living new and different lives.

Instruct participants to listen for:

- Definitions of prevenient grace.

- "Turning Points" that led the four individuals to seek transformation.

After viewing the video ask:

- What caused some of the messes that Jeanette, Mike, Jim, Kelvin, and Diana experienced in their lives? *(Responses may include: alcohol and substance abuse, physical abuse, broken families, mental illness.)*
- What was their initial response to these messes? *(Responses may include: became angry, hid the truth because of social stigmas, turned away from God, continued the cycle of inappropriate and unhealthy behavior, allowed life to spiral out of control.)*
- How did these people feel while they were living in the mess? *(Responses may include: alone, isolated from God, angry, trapped, ashamed, out of control.)*
- What were the "Turning Points" or significant realizations that led these people to seek transformation? *(Record responses on the board or the large sheet of paper you prepared with the heading "Turning Points." You will refer to these responses later in the session.)*
- What is prevenient grace? *(God's grace preceding you, running ahead of you, looking for you)*

Ask Tom Berlin's closing question from the video:

- Where have you found God to be present in your life before you were ever looking?

Bible Study and Discussion

Read, or invite someone to read, Luke 19:1-10. Ask:

- How does Jesus show love for Zacchaeus?

26

- How does Zacchaeus's acceptance of Jesus' love bless his household? *(His household receives salvation.)*
- How does Zacchaeus's acceptance of Jesus' love bless the community? *(The poor receive half of his possessions, Zacchaeus compensates those he has cheated, and the community sees a life transformed by the love of God.)*
- Who are "the lost" in our communities that Jesus "came to seek and save"?

Book Study and Discussion

Say: Early in the chapter Tom Berlin makes the point that we do not set out to create a life that is in a mess. As we have seen in the video, and as we know from our own experiences, life does not always happen as we would like it to. We sometimes find ourselves in a mess, and we ask, "How did this happen?"

Review the examples in the beginning of the chapter of the people who asked, "How did this happen?"

- The married couple who argue all the time
- The man who is aging and finds himself out of shape
- The woman who cannot hold a job

Create small groups of three or four persons. Instruct participants to keep the above three scenarios in mind, and also the stories of the four individuals in the video as they consider these questions. Ask:

- What issues do they describe that are similar to yours?
- What issues have you dealt with that may be different but are also difficult?

After the groups have had time for discussion, say:

- When we find ourselves in messy situations and we are dealing with difficult and unpleasant circumstances, it is natural to want to look back and seek answers to the question, "How did this happen?" When we look back we usually find one of three answers, or perhaps a combination of these three answers:

o   We are responsible.

o   Another person or persons are responsible.

o   We are victims of circumstances, for example an illness or natural disaster.

Participants may remain in the small groups for discussion of the following questions, or you may call the whole group back together for this discussion. Ask:

- What are helpful and healthy ways to respond if we find that we are responsible? *(Responses may include: accept responsibility, seek forgiveness, learn from our mistakes, change our behavior.)*
- What are helpful and healthy ways to respond if we find another person or group is responsible, as was the case for some of the people in the video? *(Responses may include: offer forgiveness, remove yourself from the situation.)*
- What are helpful and healthy ways to respond if we are victims of circumstances?

It is important to note that the purpose of looking back is to help us move forward. It is not helpful or healthy to "play the blame game" or "wallow in the past" or get stuck in a "poor me" attitude.

Remind participants that in dealing with a mess it's helpful to talk about the situation with others. Ask:

- Why is it so hard to talk about our problems, and how can being open with those we trust encourage and heal us?
- What are some ways people try to fix their lives without God's help?

Call attention once again to the list titled "Turning Points." Ask:

- What experiences or realizations have been turning points for you that have led you to seek transformation through Jesus Christ?
- How do these compare with the turning points we noted for the people in the video?

Sometimes Jesus seems to show up at just the right time for people. The Scripture references below tell stories that demonstrate this point.

- Mark 5:21-43: "Jesus heals two people"
- Mark 9:14-27: "A demon-possessed boy"
- Luke 7:1-10: "A servant is healed"
- John 7:53–8:11: "Pharisees test Jesus"

Choose one of the following two ways to explore these texts:

1. If there are eight or more people in your group, invite participants to form four small groups with two or more people in each group.
   o Assign each group one of the Scripture passages.
   o Provide each group with a copy of the sheet you prepared with these three questions:
      ▶ How did the person asking for healing approach Jesus?
      ▶ How do you think the person felt about approaching Jesus?
      ▶ How did Jesus respond?
   o Instruct the groups to read the Scripture references and discuss responses to the questions.
   o Call the groups back together and invite each group to share its findings.
2. If you have fewer than eight people in your group, remain together in one group and select one or two of the Scripture passages for this activity.

- o Invite volunteers to read the scripture text(s) you have selected.
- o Ask these questions for each scripture passage:
  - ► How did the person asking for healing approach Jesus?
  - ► How do you think the person felt about approaching Jesus?
  - ► How did Jesus respond?

Read, or invite a volunteer to read, the story of Jesus healing Bartimaeus, found in Mark 10:46-52. Note that Jesus asked Bartimaeus a direct question: "What do you want me to do for you?" (Mark 10:51) Note also that Bartimaeus was ready with his answer: "Teacher, I want to see." Ask:

- What is it that you want Jesus Christ to do for you? In other words, where is transformation needed in your life?
- What did Bartimaeus do when he heard that Jesus was nearby? *(See verse 47.)*
- How did bystanders respond to Bartimaeus's shouting? *(See verse 48.)*
- What did Bartimaeus do when he heard Jesus was calling him? *(See verse 50. Note that the act of "Throwing his coat to the side" might be symbolic of releasing a burden that was weighing him down, or leaving behind his old life in anticipation of the new life that Jesus could offer him.)*
- What must you throw aside before you will be ready to receive the gift of transformation?
- What did Bartimaeus do after he was healed? *(See verse 52.)*

Say: We noted in the story of Zacchaeus that the restoration of Zacchaeus's relationship with God also changed his family and his community.

Ask: How are our families, our faith communities, and our secular communities changed as we accept God's gifts of restoration and new life?

Wrapping Up

Closing Activity

Offer these summary statements:

- It is God's desire that we live in relationship with God.
- Through Christ there is a way to clean up the messes in our lives and to experience new life and reconciliation with God.
- Just as Jesus was present for Zacchaeus and Bartimaeus, Jesus is present for us.
- Just as Jesus called Zacchaeus and Bartimaeus, Jesus is calling us to experience restoration and new life with God.

Invite participants to write down these questions for personal reflection during the week:

- What do I want God to do for me?
- What is the next thing I need to do as I accept the gift of a restored relationship with God? *(For example, Zacchaeus climbed a tree, Bartimaeus jumped up, the four individuals in the video found people to talk to who could help them.)*

Closing Prayer

Great God of light, every morning your love is new, and all day long you are working for good in the world. Stir up in us desire to serve you, to live peacefully with our neighbors and all your creation, and to devote each day to your Son, our Savior Jesus Christ. Amen.

3

BLESS THIS MESS

Planning the Session

Session Goals

Through conversation, activities, and reflection, participants will consider and begin to understand the meaning of these theological concepts:

- Confession
- Forgiveness
- Justification
- Reconciliation
- Repentance
- Salvation

Biblical Foundation

- John 5:1-9

- Acts 9:1-20
- Romans 5:1-11

Before the Session

- Set up a table in the room with nametags, markers, Bibles, extra copies of *Restored,* a small stack of printer or notebook paper, and pencils.
- Have available a chalkboard and chalk, a dry-erase board and markers, or large sheets of paper and markers to record participants' responses during the session.
- Write the six words listed under Session Goals on strips of stiff paper, cardstock, or cardboard. Write one word on each strip with a bold marker, using lettering that is large enough to be seen by all participants. These will be used in the activity "Leading into the Study."
- Display a large sheet of blank paper in the room and have tape available so the six strips of paper with the words may be displayed there after the "Leading into the Study" activity.
- On the board or a large sheet of paper, write the two Greek words for life and the two Greek words for death that are mentioned in the book:
  - o *Bios*: physical, mortal life
  - o *Zoe*: spiritual, eternal life
  - o *Teleute*: physical death
  - o *Thanatos*: spiritual death

Getting Started

Opening Activities

Greet participants as they arrive. Invite everyone to make a nametag and pick up a Bible or copy of *Restored* if they did not bring one. If there are newcomers to the group, introduce yourself and allow a brief time for participants to introduce themselves.

Be sure that each participant has paper and a pen or pencil. Remind participants to covenant together that they will respect a policy of confidentiality.

Leading into the Study

The purpose of this activity is to inspire interest in the meaning of the six words listed under Session Goals and to consider the order in which they can occur in people's lives. There is not a "right" or "wrong" answer concerning the order, and some of them can happen simultaneously.

During the activity, do not offer definitions for the words. Allow conversation among participants to flow freely as they discuss what the words mean and seek to put them in order.

Before the session, determine how much time you want to allow for this activity. When you call time, let participants know that there will be more time to explore the meaning of these words throughout the session.

Introduce this activity by distributing to six volunteers the six strips you prepared with the words from the Session Goals. (You may also do this activity with three volunteers and give each volunteer two words, one to be held in each hand.)

Instruct the volunteers to stand in a row in the front of the room facing the group and to hold the words so that all participants may see them.

Say: These theological concepts are important as we seek restoration with God.

Ask: What are your ideas about the meaning of these terms?

After discussion, ask: What is the order in which these events can take place in a person's life? Keep in mind that there's not a "right" or "wrong" order, since the order can vary from person to person.

Instruct participants to arrange the words in chronological order by asking volunteers to either move to different places in the row or to exchange words. (The order may change several times during the activity.)

After a consensus is reached, ask the volunteers to tape the words to the large sheet of blank paper displayed in the room.

Opening Prayer

Loving God, sometimes we feel overwhelmed by the messes that become part of our lives. We long to change and live in a restored relationship with you. Yet, for various reasons, we sometimes hesitate to seek those changes. We sometimes choose instead to ask your blessing on the mess and settle for a life that is less than the one you desire for us. Give us wisdom and strength and courage to say no to the mess and to say yes to the abundant life you offer us. Amen.

Learning Together

Video Study and Discussion

Introduce the video by saying: The theme for this video is reconciliation. Tom Berlin invited Father Tom Murphy to share his understanding of confession and reconciliation in the Catholic tradition. As we view the video, listen especially for what is said about (1) confession, (2) community, and (3) honesty, as these relate to reconciliation.

After viewing the video, create pairs or small groups for discussion. Invite each pair or small group to share one insight from the discussion with the whole group. Ask Tom Berlin's closing question:

- Why do you think honesty is so important, and in what way is honesty absolutely essential for reconciliation?

Bible Study and Discussion

Read, or invite someone to read, John 5:1-9. Ask:

- What is the setting for this story?
- How long had the man Jesus talked with been sick?
- How did the man respond to Jesus' question, "Do you want to get well?"
- How do you respond to Jesus' question?

Book Study and Discussion

Read, or invite a volunteer to read, Acts 9:1-20. Say:

- This is the story of Saul's conversion experience.
- Each of us comes to know Jesus Christ in different ways and at different times in our lives.
- Some people pinpoint the exact date and time they came to believe in Christ. For others the process is gradual. God comes to us and grabs our attention in different ways.

Ask:

- What was Saul's life like before his conversion experience?
- How did Saul's life change after his conversion experience?

Call attention to the board or large sheet of paper you prepared that shows the Greek words for life and death.

Refer participants to the Richard Foster quotations in Chapter 3, and Tom Berlin's comments about these quotations. Ask:

- How is it possible to be "physically alive" and "spiritually dead" at the same time?
- How was Paul spiritually dead before his conversion?
- When have you felt spiritually dead? *(Note that even after we accept Jesus Christ in our lives, we may experience times when we feel separated from God.)*
- Compare the images of a short hike and a lifetime journey as they relate to the Christian life. Which is the better description? Why?

Read, or invite a volunteer to read, Romans 5:1-11. Note that some of the theological concepts listed in the opening activity are referred to in this passage.

There will be an opportunity to discuss these verses later in the session. After reading the passage, move directly to a discussion of the questions below. The comments in parentheses after the questions are discussion starters for you, not exhaustive definitions. Ask:

37

- What is confession? *(An acknowledgment of our sin. You may need to mention that confession also can mean a profession of faith or a creed.)*
- Why is honesty an important part of confession? How does confession signal a new beginning and a willingness to change?
- What is repentance? *(turning away from sin and turning toward God)* How do confession and repentance work together?
- How do you define forgiveness? *(pardon, without resentment or expected repayment of a debt)*
- Why are confession and forgiveness important in our relationships with one another as well as in our relationship with God? *(You may want to note that in the Lord's Prayer we say we will forgive others.)*
- When have you been forgiven by someone you have wronged?
- When have you forgiven someone else? How did your relationship with the other person change after confession and forgiveness?
- What is salvation? *(deliverance from the consequences of sin with the promise of eternal life)*
- What is justification? *(Being made right with God; being considered righteous in God's eyes by grace through faith. You may want to note that this is a legal term. Participants in your group who have experience in the fields of law or banking may be able to offer additional insight.)*

Note these key points:

- Forgiveness, salvation, and justification are free gifts from God, made available by God's grace.
- These are gifts that we do not deserve and cannot earn through our deeds and actions. We receive these gifts through faith, because God loves us and desires that we live in relationship with God.
- God calls us to confession and repentance so that we might have a reconciled and restored relationship with God.

- We are made in God's image. Sin has marred that image. We engage in acts of confession and repentance because we want to be restored to our original condition.

Read Romans 5:1-11 again in sections, following the outline below. Invite volunteers to read each section, and you or they can note variations in translation.

Read Romans 5:1-2. Ask:

- What does it mean to be "justified" (NRSV and NIV) or "made righteous" (CEB)? *(to be put in a right relationship with God)*
- Who makes our justification or righteousness possible?
- What do we receive as a result of justification?

Read Romans 5:3-4. Ask:

- What do these verses tell us about the value of asking God to help us work through our messes—that is, our "suffering" (NRSV and NIV) or the "problems" and "trouble" (CEB) in our lives?
- How have you experienced the progression from "endurance" to "character" to "hope"?

Read Romans 5:6-11. Ask:

- What are some of the benefits we have received through the death of Christ? *(justification, righteousness, salvation, reconciliation, restoration)*
- How do you think Christ's sacrifice of his life proved that God loves us?
- In what ways does this Scripture text from Romans offer you encouragement to "confess the mess" and ask God to change your life and restore the image of God within you?
- In what ways have you already experienced what Tom Berlin identifies as the transforming power of God?

Wrapping Up

Closing Activity

This lesson covered a lot of material and may have stirred up a variety of feelings among the participants. Ask:

- How are you feeling now after our discussion of Chapter 3? *(Responses may include: overwhelmed, confused, hesitant, encouraged, reassured, and motivated.)*

Say: God has already prepared for our reconciliation and restoration through his Son, Jesus Christ. God calls us to:

- identify and confess our sin;
- repent and turn toward God.

Offer this idea for personal reflection during the week. Say:

- Try writing a letter to God. Only you and God will see the letter unless you choose to share it with someone else, so you may be completely open and honest. Use the letter as an opportunity to:
  o   confess your sin;
  o   consider changes you would like to see in your life;
  o   ask God to change and transform you.

Spend time in silent prayer and listen for God's response to your letter.

Closing Prayer

God of love and grace, God of healing and forgiveness, God of restoration and hope, thank you! Thank you for the gift of salvation through your son, Jesus Christ. Open our hearts to you so that we may openly and honestly confess our sin and identify the messes that need to be changed in our lives. Thank you for the assurance of your forgiveness. Thank you for your faithful presence that is always with us as we journey toward restoration. Amen.

4

NO MESSING AROUND

Planning the Session

Session Goals

Through conversation, activities, and reflection, participants will begin to:

- Consider what it means to live a restored life with God:
  o It does not mean living with less mess.
  o It requires that we stop "messing around" in an old life.
  o It means living a completely new life in Christ.
- Discover the blessings of the new life that Christ offers us.

Biblical Foundation

- Colossians 3:1-17

Before the Session

- Set up a table in the room with nametags, markers, Bibles, extra copies of *Restored*, a small stack of printer or notebook paper, and pencils.
- Have available a chalkboard and chalk, a dry-erase board and markers, or large sheets of paper and markers to record participants' responses during the session.
- Cut out small paper hearts, enough for each person to have three or four for an activity during the Book Study and Discussion. Also draw the outline of a heart on a large sheet of paper and display it in the room. Have tape available so participants may attach the small hearts inside the outline.
- A few days before the session, recruit two or three participants to share their experiences of new birth or the presence and power of the Holy Spirit in their lives. Ask participants to limit their comments to two or three minutes. This activity is included under Book Study and Discussion.

Getting Started

Opening Activities

Greet participants as they arrive. Invite everyone to make a nametag if these are still necessary. If there are newcomers to the group, introduce yourself and allow a brief time for participants to introduce themselves. Remind participants of the covenant to respect a policy of confidentiality.

Leading into the Study

Remind participants of the title for this session, "No Messing Around." Note Tom Berlin's point that living a restored life requires that we stop "messing around" in our old life. Ask:

- Why might it be tempting to hold on to aspects of an old life even after we have decided we want a new life in Christ?

- When you backslide, as all of us do, how do you respond? What are some ways in which you try to make it right?

Opening Prayer

Holy God, your Son gave his all for us so that we might have a reconciled and restored relationship with you. Show us how to turn away from sin and the mess in our lives. Show us the way to live a completely new life in Christ. Thank you for your love and grace, which invite us into a restored relationship with you. Amen.

Learning Together

Video Study and Discussion

Introduce the video by saying: In the video this week, we revisit our friends from Session 2 who recognized the mess in their lives and knew they needed to change. This week, we learn how their lives have transformed since turning to God.

Invite participants to listen for what the individuals say about:

- What they needed to do in order for the healing process to work;
- What their lives are like today.

After viewing the video, ask:

- What did these individuals need to be willing to do before the healing process could begin? *(confess their sins, let go of fear and pride, share their situations with others, accept encouragement, surrender control to God)*
- How did the lives of these individuals change after they accepted God's healing and help?
- Why is the recovery process easier for a person who has faith in God?

Ask Tom Berlin's closing questions from the video:

- If you want to gain a new life in Christ, you have to surrender the old one, and that is not easy to do. Where do you struggle with that? Where do you struggle to let go of control in your life in such a way that God can really begin to transform you?

Bible Study and Discussion

Read, or invite volunteers to read, Colossians 3:1-17 in sections as outlined below. Allow time for discussion of the accompanying questions after each section is read.

Read Colossians 3:1-4. Ask:

- How do you think looking above to the risen Christ can lead us to a new restored life with God?

Read Colossians 3:5-11. Ask:

- What "practices" are part of "the old human nature"? What are your thoughts about these?

Read Colossians 3:12-17. Ask:

- What characterizes "the new nature"? (*Note that the "new nature" conforms to God's image.*)
- How does focusing on the good things listed in verses 12-15 help us deal with the sins listed in verses 5-10?

Book Study and Discussion

Say: When we take the first step and decide that we want to live within a restored relationship with God, God is there for us. When we decide we no longer want to mess around in our old life, God is ready to guide us on our journey from the old to the new. God is ready to help us "Take off the old human nature . . . and put on the new nature"

(Colossians 3:9-10). God is ready for us to know the joy of a restored relationship with Him.

Offer a few minutes of silence for participants to reflect on the following questions. Suggest that participants refer back to Colossians 3:5-17 and the letters to God that they may have written during the week (see the closing activity for Session 3) as they consider their responses.

Questions for personal reflection:

- What do you need to let go of or turn away from in order to know a restored relationship with God?
- What fears and worries would you like to release to God?
- What do you need to surrender to God before restoration can take place?

Distribute three or four paper hearts to each person and invite participants to write on these hearts their responses to the questions above, and then to attach the hearts within the heart shape on the large sheet of paper. (If you chose not to make the hearts, then instruct participants to write their responses in their notebooks.)

After this time of silent reflection, suggest that participants refer to their responses frequently and pray for God's help as they release these things to God. Then offer this prayer:

Merciful God, you know the desires of our hearts. Grant us strength as we turn away from these things that separate us from you. Grant us an overwhelming consciousness of your presence and love. Amen.

Say: Imagine your life without the sins, fears, and worries you wrote about in the previous activity. Tom Berlin suggests that if those were suddenly gone, "you would feel a weight fall off your shoulders. You would have less pain and guilt in your life. You would be more joyful. Others would enjoy being around you more. It would be a gift."

Create discussion groups of three to five people. Ask:

- Why is it difficult to surrender control of our lives to God?
- What characteristics of "the new nature" as described in Colossians 3:12-17 do you already possess or practice?
- What characteristics of "the new nature" do you want to practice or possess in your life?
- What are some things you can do to make these characteristics part of who you are? *(Responses may include the spiritual disciplines of worship, Bible study, prayer, and service.)*
- What blessings and gifts do we experience when we align our lives with God's plan for us?

Call the group back together. Recall that the people who shared their stories in the video acknowledged that placing their faith in Christ did not mean they no longer struggled with some aspects of their former lives. Ask:

- What are examples of conditions, situations, or temptations that might not change when a person finds new life in Christ? *(Examples include: physical or mental disabilities, temptation toward an addictive behavior, a challenging work environment, a person with whom we have difficulty getting along.)*
- How does our faith in Christ help us face these challenges and live in these environments in a new way?
- What gifts does God offer us when we surrender control of our lives to God? *(Responses may include: continued presence, guidance, wisdom, strength, courage, forgiveness, and peace.)*
- What are some signs that warn us we are falling back into old patterns and seeking to take back control of our lives? What are some ways we can guard against these?

Invite participants to turn to the section of the chapter titled "The Cross." Ask:

- What are some of the cross's meanings for humankind? *(You may want to record responses on a chalkboard or dry-erase board or a large sheet or paper.)*

Invite a volunteer to summarize the story of Nicodemus in the chapter section titled "Nicodemus's Questions."

Read these two verses from the story of Nicodemus in the Gospel of John:

- Jesus answered, "I assure you, unless someone is born anew, it's not possible to see God's kingdom." (John 3:3)
- Jesus answered, "I assure you, unless someone is born of water and the Spirit, it's not possible to enter God's kingdom." (John 3:5)

Ask:

- What does it mean to be "born of water and the Spirit"?
- What role does baptism play in the life of a follower of Christ?
- How is the image of new birth a helpful symbol as we seek to understand what it means to move from our old life to the new life God offers us?

Invite the two or three people you recruited ahead of time to briefly share their experiences of new birth or the presence of the Holy Spirit. If time permits you may invite others to share briefly.

Be mindful that some participants in the group may not feel that they have experienced new birth or the presence of the Holy Spirit in their lives. Offer encouragement that taking this course is a great first step toward experiencing new birth and a restored relationship with God.

Ask participants to consider baptism and discuss the following questions.

- In our tradition, what does baptism consist of?
- What promises are made by or on behalf of the person being baptized?
- What does the pastor call upon God to do?
- What words and symbols represent new birth and transformation?

Wrapping Up

Closing Activity

Read Galatians 5:22-25.

> But the fruit of the Spirit is love, joy, peace, patience, kindness, goodness, faithfulness, gentleness, and self-control. There is no law against things like this. Those who belong to Christ Jesus have crucified the self with its passions and its desires. If we live by the Spirit, let's follow the Spirit.

Call attention to the closing section of the book chapter, titled "The Vine." Invite participants to reflect on these two questions during the week.

- How are you following Paul's direction to "follow the Spirit"?
- How are you like a vine reaching for God? What other metaphors seem to fit our seeking to follow the Spirit?

Closing Prayer

Holy and loving God, thank you for the promise of new birth and new life in Christ. We desire to experience transformation in order to be restored to a right relationship with you, so that we will reflect your image within us. Guide our steps as we live this lifelong journey. Inspire us to take the first step and then keep on taking the next steps as we grow in faith and love. Amen.

5

ADDRESS THIS MESS

Planning the Session

Session Goals

Through conversation, activities, and reflection, participants will begin to:

- Understand the meaning of sanctifying grace and humility;
- Recognize the need for spiritual disciplines to keep us connected to God;
- Consider the value of spiritual disciplines they practice;
- Explore new spiritual disciplines they want to incorporate into their lives.

Biblical Foundation

- Luke 10:38-42
- Luke 11:9

Before the Session

- Set up a table in the room with nametags, markers, Bibles, extra copies of *Restored,* a small stack of printer or notebook paper, and pencils.
- Have available a chalkboard and chalk, a dry-erase board and markers, or large sheets of paper and markers to record participants' responses during the session.
- Write the numbers one through twenty in a vertical column along the left side of the board or a large sheet of paper. Leave room after each number to write a response from the group. This will be used for the Leading into the Study activity.
- Write the word *perispao* on the board or a large sheet of paper and display it in the room. You may want to use colored markers or embellished lettering so it will stand out.
- Write the headings "Disciplines of Abstinence" and "Disciplines of Engagement" on the board or on large sheets of paper for use in group discussion.
- Make three copies of the instructions and questions for the activity "What Does Jesus Say?" to distribute to the three small groups, or write the instructions and questions on the board or a large sheet of paper.
- For the closing activity, choose a hymn about the Holy Spirit in advance or get copies of your church hymnal to distribute to the group if you would like them to choose the hymn. Have Internet printouts of the lyrics for group members if you don't distribute hymnals.

Getting Started

Opening Activities

Greet participants as they arrive. Invite everyone to make a nametag if these are still necessary. If there are newcomers to the group, introduce yourself and allow a brief time for participants to introduce themselves. Remind participants of the covenant to respect a policy of confidentiality.

Leading into the Study

Call attention to the board or large sheet of paper you have prepared with the column of numbers one through twenty. Recruit a volunteer to record the first twenty responses from the group. Ask:

- What are some of the things you did yesterday? *(Instruct participants to call out the first activities that come to mind until you reach twenty.)*

You may want to record responses to the following questions on another board or large sheet of paper. Ask:

- What did you plan to do but not have time to do?
- What did you forget to do? Why did you forget?

Refer back to the list of twenty activities as participants respond to the questions below. Circle any responses that are on the list. Add any responses that are not on the list. Ask:

- What activities brought you joy?
- What did you do that helped you feel closer to God?

Say: There are many distractions in the world that can draw us away from God. We need to be intentional about engaging in activities that can help us stay connected with God. During this session, think about your own connection with God and consider ways you might work toward strengthening that connection.

Opening Prayer

Loving God, when you created the world you brought order to chaos. You created us in your image so that we might be connected to you. Yet sometimes, Lord, we wander away. We become distracted by many things that call for our attention. Then we become lost and feel separated from you, and our lives end up in a mess. Merciful God, we do not want to live in the mess. We want to be restored to you and to remain with you. Grant us courage as we step out in faith. Amen. Learning Together

Learning Together

Video Study and Discussion

Introduce the video by simply saying, "We are going tandem sky-diving." After viewing the video ask:

- How did you feel in those moments before Tom Berlin jumped out of the airplane?
- How did you feel when he and his instructor were in freefall before the parachute opened?
- How did you feel after the parachute opened?

Note Tom Berlin's point that we are sometimes forced to take plunges that we do not choose. Exaples may include a frightening medical diagnosis, financial uncertainty, or a broken relationship. Ask:

- When have you been plunged into a situation where you had no control and you needed to surrender control to someone else?
- How did you feel in that situation?

Ask Tom Berlin's closing questions from the video:

- How is it going? Do you feel connected, and which connections are making the difference in relieving your fears?

Bible Study and Discussion

Read, or invite someone to read, Luke 10:38-42. Note that the people in Jesus' day placed great value on hospitality. Ask:

- How do you show hospitality to visitors in your home?
- What do you do to prepare for someone's visit?
- In what ways do your preparations and the work of hospitality distract you from being present with your guests after they arrive?
- What is "necessary" when serving as a host, and what is "the better part" that Jesus speaks of? Which do you find yourself doing when you have guests?
- What did Jesus mean when he said, "It won't be taken away from her"?

Invite a volunteer to read or summarize the story in Chapter 5 attributed to Tom Long about a mission trip to Jamaica.

Highlight the last two sentences of that story: "I think that teacher had been like Mary, sitting at Jesus' feet. And because she had, she could get up like Martha and teach those children with joy and hope, seeing Jesus in the face of every one of them."

Book Study and Discussion

Invite participants to refer to the sections of the chapter titled "Sanctifying Grace" and "The Power of Humility" as they respond to these questions. Ask:

- What is sanctifying grace?
- How have you experienced sanctifying grace in your life?
- What is humility?
- Where are you on the journey of humility?

Call attention to the word *perispao* displayed in the room. Ask:

- What does this Greek word mean? *(See the explanation in Chapter 5.)*
- What causes us to suffer from *perispao*?
- How do distractions in our lives draw us away from God?

- What happens when we try to transform our lives on our own?

Invite participants to share responses to the next three questions in pairs or groups of three. Depending on time available you may want to encourage participants to be concise in their responses. Ask:

- When was a time when distractions drew you away from God?
- What were the warning signs that you were feeling disconnected from God? What did you do to reconnect?

Conclude this conversation by noting that spiritual practices or disciplines offer a way for us to reconnect and stay connected to God. Read these words of Richard Foster as quoted in *Restored*:

> God freely and graciously invites us to participate in this transforming process. But not on our own.[1]

Record responses to the following questions on a board or large sheet of paper: Ask:

- What are "Disciplines of Abstinence"? *(solitude, silence, frugality, chastity, secrecy, sacrifice)*
- What are "Disciplines of Engagement"? *(study, worship, celebration, service, prayer, fellowship, confession)*[2]

Say: As we have explored the subject of restoration with God, we have seen that our commitment to seek and accept the gift of restoration plays a big role in the process. At some point we have to move from the desire to change to the practices that lead to change. We have to move from asking God to bless the mess to figuring out how, with God's help, we can address the mess.

What Does Jesus Say?

Create three small groups and assign Scripture texts to each:

- Group 1: Matthew 5:1-9, 13-16
- Group 2: Matthew 6:1-34
- Group 3: Matthew 7:1-28

Instruct each group to

1. Silently skim the passage assigned to their group.
2. Discuss responses to these questions:
   o What is Jesus instructing us to do?
   o How can these instructions become spiritual practices that draw us closer to God?
3. Select three spiritual practices from the Scripture text to share with the larger group.

Distribute copies of these instructions to each group or call attention to the board or large sheet of paper where you wrote the instructions before the session. Let the groups know how much time they will have to complete this activity.

After the allotted time has passed, call the groups back together to share their findings. On the board or a large sheet of paper, make a list of the various spiritual practices as they are mentioned by each group.

After each group has shared, call attention to the lists of "Disciplines of Abstinence" and "Disciplines of Engagement." Ask:

- Which of these spiritual practices are examples of "Disciplines of Abstinence": solitude, silence, frugality, chastity, secrecy, sacrifice?
- Which of these spiritual practices are examples of "Disciplines of Engagement": study, worship, celebration, service, prayer, fellowship, confession?
- What spiritual practices or disciplines do you find helpful in your daily life?
- Where do you feel you consistently do the will of God and follow Jesus' teaching?

- Where do you struggle to put Jesus' words into practice?
- What new spiritual practices or disciplines would you like to incorporate into your life?

Wrapping Up

Closing Activity

Note Tom Berlin's comment: "It's worth noting that the first word used for God in Genesis 1 is *Ruach*, a Hebrew term meaning the air, wind, or Spirit of God. Spiritual practices enable us to take in the breath of heaven and find renewal as a result."

Say: Spiritual practices offer a way for us to connect with the Holy Spirit and experience renewal, restoration, and transformation in our lives.

Select an activity below. Distribute hymnals (for Option 1) or Internet printouts of lyrics (for Option 2).

1. Invite participants to look in the hymnal for hymns related to the Holy Spirit. Allow a few minutes for participants to share phrases from the hymns that they find meaningful and helpful, then sing or read the words together.
2. Invite participants to look at the hymn about the Holy Spirit that you have selected ahead of time. Sing or read the words together.

Closing Prayer

Lord, lead us to your Spirit through prayer, through silence, and through service. Help us look and listen for the Holy Spirit in our lives, so that we may align ourselves more closely with you and restore your image within us. In Jesus' name we pray. Amen.

6

THE MESSAGE IN THE MESS

Planning the Session

Session Goals

Through conversation, activities, and reflection, participants will begin to:

- Discern the meaning of sanctification;
- Identify ways to remain connected to God.

Biblical Foundation

Matthew 22:34-40
Philippians 1:6

Before the Session

- Set up a table in the room with nametags, markers, Bibles, extra copies of *Restored,* a small stack of printer or notebook paper, and pencils.

- Have available a chalkboard and chalk, a dry-erase board and markers, or large sheets of paper and markers to record participants' responses during the session.
- Make two columns on the board or a large sheet of paper. Write the heading "Dents" in the first column and the heading "Restored" in the second column. This will be used for the "Leading into the Study" activity.

Getting Started

Opening Activities

Greet participants as they arrive. Invite everyone to make a nametag if these are still necessary. If there are newcomers to the group, introduce yourself and allow a brief time for participants to introduce themselves. Remind participants of the covenant to respect a policy of confidentiality.

Leading into the Study

Say: Remember that the first session of this study was titled, "This Is a Real Mess." The setting for the video was a junkyard filled with wrecked vehicles. During this study we have talked about what it means to be made in God's image. We have explored reasons why God's image within us becomes covered up. We have been invited to accept God's gift of restoration so that we can be the people God intends us to be.

Call attention to the board or paper you've prepared that has two columns: "Dents" and "Restored." Ask:

- Where are the "dents" and brokenness in your life that cover the image of God within you?
- What would your restored life with God look like?

(These are personal questions and you may want to remind participants that sharing is optional. It is hoped that participants have developed a level of trust as a result of journeying through these sessions together.)

Opening Prayer

Holy God, you have created us in your image and called us to be holy. When we seek to live life on our own, your image within us gets covered up by our sin and fear. We need your help to be holy, your help to reach perfection in Christ. We open our hearts to you. We confess our sin and seek your forgiveness. Open our eyes that we may see "The Message in the Mess." Grant us the wisdom to accept your grace and follow you. Amen.

Learning Together

Video Study and Discussion

Introduce the video by saying: We saw a junkyard in the video for Session 1, and today we'll go to a garage where a car has been restored. As you watch, think about ways in which restoring a car is similar to restoring a person, and ways in which it is different.

After the video, ask:

- Why did Dan join a car club when he decided to restore his car? What benefits and blessings did Dan receive from the people who offered help?
- How does Dan's restored car enhance his life in a way that his unrestored car could not?
- Who may we go to for help when we seek a restored relationship with God? What blessings have you received from people who have helped you grow closer to God?
- How does a restored life bring you joy?

Ask Tom Berlin's closing question from the video:

- What do you need to do if you are going to experience "full restoration"?

Bible Study and Discussion

Read, or invite someone to read, Philippians 1:6: "I'm sure about this: the one who started a good work in you will stay with you to complete the job by the day of Christ Jesus." Ask:

- What "good work" has God started in you?
- What do you think "the day of Christ Jesus" means?
- What feelings do you experience when you read that God "will stay with you to complete the job"?
- When you read this verse, do you feel called to make changes in your life? If so, what changes?

Book Study and Discussion

Note Tom Berlin's point in the section titled "Getting Serious about the Message" that God desires complete restoration and transformation in our lives, not a patchwork job. Ask for a volunteer to read the last paragraph in this section of the book:

> Right now you may be thinking, This book must be for other people. He can't be talking about me. But the Bible's message is that Jesus' death and resurrection happened for nothing less than the sanctification of all who would follow him. Sanctification, complete sanctification, in which you are fully formed and owned by God's love, will reveal that you are in fact a masterpiece.

- Do you find it hard to believe that Tom Berlin is talking about you? Why or why not?
- What does sanctification mean? How does sanctifying grace relate to the two kinds of grace we discussed earlier: prevenient grace and justifying grace?
- Try to imagine the masterpiece that God is making in you. Even if it's hard to imagine, try to describe a detail or two.

Invite participants to tell about a person they know who has a close relationship with God. Ask:

- What spiritual disciplines does this person follow to remain closely connected with God?

Remind participants that love is at the heart of the Christian message. Read, or invite someone to read, Matthew 22:34-40. Ask:

- What are some things we can do to move us toward the goal of loving God and neighbor?
- Where do we need God's help as we journey toward this goal to love? *(Responses may include: forgiving a person who is difficult to forgive, moving past a prejudice, putting others' needs before our own.)*
- What are some ways in which we can rely on God's power and the work of the Holy Spirit in our lives as we seek to fulfill the commandment to love?

Invite volunteers to read the Scripture texts below. Select volunteers with different versions of the Bible to read the same text for comparison.

Psalm 119:10-11. Ask:

- How did the psalmist seek to remain faithful and receive the gift of sanctification?

2 Timothy 1:9. Ask:

- What does this Scripture passage teach us about sanctification?

Invite participants to refer to the section of the book titled "What's the Alternative?" Select a volunteer to retell the story of Nadeem. Ask:

- What did you learn about yourself from Nadeem's story?
- How do you respond to Nadeem's question: "What's the alternative? If I choose not to love my enemies, what am I choosing instead? Bitterness? Revenge? Rage? Do any of these look good to you?"

Share these words of Jesus: "If a house is divided against itself, that house cannot stand" (Mark 3:25 NIV). Ask:

- When have you experienced a struggle within yourself between sin and honoring God?
- What are some warning signs that your spiritual life may be experiencing "entropy" or losing energy?

Record responses to the following two questions on the board or a large sheet of paper.

- What are some ways to breathe new energy into your growing relationship with God?
- How might you incorporate the idea of "continual engagement" in your life as a way of staying connected with God?

Invite a volunteer to retell the story of the boy flying his kite at the beach. Remind participants that "wind" is an image for the Holy Spirit. Note Tom Berlin's comment that "you have to give up trying to be the wind. You have to go where the wind is found" Ask:

- When have you tried to be the wind for yourself? What happened?
- Where can we find the wind that is God's presence and power in the Holy Spirit?

Wrapping Up

Closing Activity

Note that Tom Berlin suggests four ways that we can be assured of the power of sanctifying grace working within us and transforming us. These are:

- We trust in God's love.
- We are confident in God's ability.
- We believe in God's future.
- We believe we can be perfected in love.

Invite participants to consider those four statements as "I" statements.

- I trust in God's love.
- I am confident in God's ability.
- I believe in God's future.
- I believe I can be perfected in love.

For each of the "I" statements, offer the following questions for personal reflection:

- Does this statement describe me 100 percent?
- If yes, how?
- If no, why not? What would the percentage be? Why am I doubting?

As you bring this group study to a close, offer these words of encouragement:

- Growing in faith and our relationship with God is a lifelong journey.
- God forgives us and offers us new opportunities to start over when we stumble.
- We can trust in God's constant presence and love.

Encourage participants to incorporate spiritual disciplines into their daily lives and to share their struggles and progress with trusted friends and mentors as they continue to grow in a restored and transformed relationship with God.

Closing Prayer

Holy and generous God, we thank you for your amazing gifts of love and grace. We thank you for the gift of sanctifying grace and the joy of living a holy life. Guide us on our journeys of faith. Help us keep our eyes on Jesus Christ so that we will learn from his example. Fill us with the power of your Holy Spirit so we may have the courage and wisdom we need to follow you. Open our eyes to the needs of those around us so that we may share the good news of your love and grace with others. Amen.

NOTES

Session 5

1. Richard J. Foster, "Salvation Is for Life," Theology Today 61 (2004), 303 (https://hopekaibear.files.wordpress.com/2008/05/salvationisforlife1 .pdf).

2. On the Disciplines of Abstinence and Engagement, see Dallas Willard, *The Spirit of the Disciplines: Understanding How God Changes Lives* (New York: HarperCollins, 1991), 158.